The Pleiades at Dawn

The Pleiades at Dawn

A Tanka Collection
by
Jeanne Emrich

LONE EGRET PRESS

The Pleiades at Dawn
A Tanka Collection by Jeanne Emrich

Copyright © 2007 by Jeanne Emrich

ISBN 0-9766407-2-4

Cover painting by Jeanne Emrich

First printing, January 1, 2007

Published by
LONE EGRET PRESS
6566 France Avenue South, Ste. 1210
Edina, Minnesota 55435
USA

Produced by
BLACK CAT PRESS
613 Okemo Drive
Eldersburg, Maryland 21784
USA

Manufactured in the United States of America

In memory
of
George J. Emrich

Foreword

Jeanne Emrich is a contemporary American poet and *The Pleiades at Dawn* is her first published collection of English tanka.

Tanka, meaning "short song," is the modern name for a form of lyric verse which originated in Japan more than 1,300 years ago, and which continues to be honored and practiced as the epitome of Japanese poetry. Known until the early twentieth century as *waka*, or "Japanese song," this poetic genre has retained the same classical structure throughout its long, long history. Briefly, tanka is a largely unpunctuated, unrhymed verse form of thirty-one Japanese syllables, or sound units. As there are no poetic stress accents in Japanese, tanka are given rhythm by writing to a short/long/short/long/long pattern of 5/7/5/7/7 sound-unit phrases, with varying breath pauses being made when read aloud.

Japanese waka/tanka first became known in the West through various translations published from around 100 years ago. Following the appearance of this poetry in translation, some non-Japanese poets began to experiment with writing their own versions of it. Initially, those who designated their compositions as tanka tended to apply the same syllabic rules as their Japanese counterparts. However, in recent times research has proved that, due to inherent differences between the two languages, English tanka of thirty-one syllables not only seem heavier and more wordy than Japanese tanka, but actually take longer to be read aloud. Accordingly, it has been postulated that English tanka of twenty-one syllables, plus or minus, best approximate the Japanese model.

On this basis, and while seeking to use their own particular creativity, poets like Jeanne Emrich, who are writing now, for the most part do not keep to the fixed syllabification and patterning of Japanese tankaists, or to a particular metrical beat.

At the same time, the majority of English tanka, including Emrich's, are conventionally presented in a five-line form, which mirrors the five phrases of Japanese tanka, and which distinguishes them from brief free-verse compositions.

Jeanne Emrich is an artist and a fine poet to date better known for her compositions in the *haiku* form as well as in *haiga*, or poem-painting. Haiku, initially called "hokku," evolved in Japan some 400 years ago from the opening seventeen syllables of the "renga," a longer form of linked verses, which itself was created as an extension of traditional tanka. During the latter part of the twentieth century, haiku attained worldwide recognition and popularity. However, other than in Japan, where the study and writing of tanka thrive and tanka material maintain a mass market, this genre has been slower to establish itself in contemporary literature.

Over the last thirty or forty years, tanka has been gaining ground and has gradually come to be acknowledged as an important form of poetry internationally. The greater length of tanka enables the poet to express her/his ideas and feelings to an extent not possible within the fundamentally objective three phrases of conventional haiku. In *The Pleiades at Dawn*, Jeanne Emrich has shown herself capable of making a seamless transition from haiku to tanka composition. Traditionally untitled, tanka are essentially fragmentary; hence, as in this current collection, they are appropriately presented in English without initial capitalization or final periods.

Emrich's work clearly reflects the definition given of tanka by the most famous female Japanese poet of modern times, Yosano Akiko (1878–1942), that "it is a poem with a middle only; its beginning lies in the poet's actual experience, and its end, if any, has to be sought in the reader's mind. It is a piece of life captured verbally."

The often-quoted preface to the *Kokinshû*, a Japanese imperial anthology from the tenth century, states that tanka (then known as waka) is "poetry which effortlessly moves the heavens and the earth, awakens the world of invisible spirits to deep feelings, softens the relationship between men and women and consoles the hearts of fierce warriors." Thus tanka can, and do, address any subject which engages our senses and our emotions. Nonetheless, the greater proportion of tanka has always encompassed poems of love, love in all aspects and contexts.

The Pleiades at Dawn, while being a thoroughly modern collection, fits beautifully within the love tradition. Its very title poem echoes the legacy of longing and loss from Japanese court poetry of more than 1,000 years ago:

> *how was I to know*
> *it would end like this?*
> *the Pleiades at dawn*
> *and your hand come to rest*
> *on the small of my back*

11

The same wistful, almost elegiac, tone winds through this collection of tanka. In many, the subject and persona are left vague; such tanka can be read as referring to anyone dear to Emrich, not necessarily to the stylized lover of romantic poetry.

While love tanka are predominant in *The Pleiades at Dawn*, Emrich's questioning nature finds graceful expression also, in some existentialist poems—like her farewell, *"am I to end in dust?...."*

At the same time, as in the best contemporary tanka in any language, Emrich's surroundings and specific situation are made apparent here and there: one piece commences, *"undetected/by airport security...."*

Amongst reminiscences and poetic probings, one finds delightful surprises: *"...even at this age/I contemplate a tattoo/only a lover would see"*.

The Pleiades at Dawn is a truly engaging collection. Jeanne Emrich is to be warmly congratulated on her exciting tanka debut.

Amelia Fielden, poet and Japanese translator

today my heart
is a white magnolia
in early spring
I do not hesitate
to risk everything

swimming alone
I make of you
a virtual lover...
water curling around
my slender waist

like two mirrors
facing one another
we stare
until both of us disappear
in each other's eyes

finding my pages
in her scrapbook
I remember
the snapshots more
than the child I was

once ocean-scented
these postcards mailed
long ago
when you thought
even the sand was new

peering
into the lily's throat—
what might I have been
had our ancestors
not parted company?

in the pre-dawn darkness
a sense of the cosmos
creating itself...
I wait in the kitchen
for the tea water to boil

how was I to know
it would end like this?
the Pleiades at dawn
and your hand come to rest
on the small of my back

still fresh
from last night's dream
I walk the beach
to see what part of itself
the tide has shed

finding
your letter left out
in the rain...
if not for that small remorse
I might have forgotten you

though bars of light
fall across this pen
my words escape
like butterflies
too small for a cage

polishing
the picture window
without you
I shut the curtains
on a too-large sunset

how long has it been
since we parted?
the snow has come
and I'm learning from geese
how to fall from the sky

melting snow gurgles
in the little creek—
you tell a joke
and already I'm laughing
before the punch line

one last sliver of light
falls across the frozen pond—
I walk home at twilight
remembering you and
how I loved your shadows

the door propped open—
we trudge in with
one wet box after another;
our new house begins its life
in a blizzard

so as not to waken you
I feel my way in the dark—
the upstairs hallway
its own little universe
of windows and doors

we walked the beach
mother and daughter—
how I wish
it was you who found
that perfect sand dollar

summer solstice...
the hint of lavender
in her empty room
vanishes
the moment I notice

after the soap bubbles
we go inside—
the March wind
having stolen what's left
of your childhood

gone now
from the stubble field
your laughter
as you ran tossing
corn cobs in the air

not thinking really
I just roll paint
over five years of your life
and admire how it
freshens up the room

hardly any dust
in this sparkling house—
I think of Picasso
who let it pile up
on every painting

straight to bed
after hours in the kitchen...
what will he make of it?
the scent of cinnamon
on my fingers

events of the day
crowd around me...
I'd fall asleep
if only one night bird
would awaken and sing

autumn in Paris...
after leaving the bookstore
loved by Hemingway
I write a poem on a leaf
for the river to read

undetected
by airport security
a tiny leaf
stuck to my sandal
from our walk together

don't take me
into your old age
with you, mother—
even the waning moon
keeps its distance

did the young girl
she once was
slip back into her body?
I saw her on my mother's face
as she lay dying

you run laughing
with your brother piggyback
through the waves
just so carry me someday
when I am old

the door left open
to your childhood room
I play on the piano
a minuet Mozart composed
when he was six

his life story
along this cobble beach
interrupted
by each agate we dig up
with our toes

the soft light
of a summer constellation
gleams on the patio...
if he were alive
we'd be sitting there

plucking
the last grape on the vine
without sin or seed
our season
of small pleasures

summer's end...
I let my hair air dry
remembering a girl
who once came laughing
out of sun-splashed waters

at her gravesite
with head bowed
I think of her talent
for ripening peaches
to perfection

long winter hours...
in my parents' absence
I feel the "his" and "hers"
slip away from the humidor,
the sewing machine

winter solstice...
I toss recent snapshots
in with the old—
a drawer full of relatives
who never met

suddenly warm...
little avalanches of snow
fall from our roof
the weight of winter dreams
too heavy to bear

why do I feel
so empty tonight?
moonlight streams in
at every window
and you await me

after love-making
the darkness of our bed—
I console myself
even stars move away
from the center

there it is again—
that feeling of floating
alone in outer space
and all I did was
open your door

for breakfast
we eat our eggs
without salt
starting our day with
tiny, lopsided smiles

leaving you
after so long
like a zoo-born lion
I thought the cage
was my skin

do I forgive you?
yes I forgive you
the way rock
forgives lichen or
fallow fields the plow

the day I left
that grandfather clock
your never repaired
rang once, or so
I imagined

the sunset has moved
to a different window—
what shall I say
to the child
still mourning?

just when I think
I have forgotten him
I open my mouth to sing
and out comes
his voice

lingering
at the shop window—
even at this age
I contemplate a tattoo
only a lover would see

age, you say,
is a matter of mind—
outside my window
a monarch birch still
peeling layers of itself

wondering for years
what would be
my life's defining moment—
an egret staring at me
me staring back

do I live in this world?
last night, I am told,
the crickets
droned their last
and I never heard

the way winter leaves
cling to the red oak—
all I know for sure
is the easy questions
were answered long ago

dry seeds scatter
from my hand into the wind—
one clings
as if to say there is in me
something yet to be

with these words
I make a feast
in honor of lost days—
fallen grasses pointing
their light into the snow

am I to end as dust?
very well, let me float
in the morning sunlight
set me aswirl
with your laughter

Acknowledgments

I would like to thank Cathy Drinkwater Better for her encouragement and enthusiasm in support of the formation of this book, her thoughtful editorial assistance, and finally, her considerable expertise and professionalism in all phases of production. I also greatly appreciate the production assistance of Cathy's husband, Doug Walker. Warm thanks to Michael McClintock for his early readings of the manuscript and his hearty endorsement of it and also to Amelia Fielden for writing a fine foreword, including an excellent introduction to tanka, its history and aesthetics. Finally, my gratitude to Jane and Werner Reichhold for the inspiration and many opportunities they have provided to poets in the West to learn, flourish, and ultimately shine with this form. You have led the way and you continue to do so!

A number of the verses within this collection were included in my tanka play, *Second Chance* (2005), with dance and jazz sax accompaniment, and also in *Fallen Grasses* (2006), with a choral composition by Susan Precourt Reddin; both were performed at the Bloomington Fine Arts Center, Minnesota. Many verses have been published in *The Tanka Anthology: Tanka in English and from Around the World* (Red Moon Press, 2003), and in such journals as: *American Tanka*; *Ribbons: Journal of the Tanka Society of America*; *red lights*; *gusts: Contemporary Tanka* (Canada); *Tangled Hair* (United Kingdom); *Hermitage* (Romania); and such online journals as: *LYNX: A Journal for Linking Poets*; and *Modern English Tanka*. "how long has it been" earned First Place in the 2005 San Francisco International Tanka Competition.

About the Poet

Jeanne Emrich is a poet and artist living in Edina, Minnesota. She became interested in Japanese culture and poetry forms in 1995 after moving to a new house and discovering a Japanese garden nearby. She has written haiku, tanka, renku, and contemporary haiga or poem-paintings. She was the founder and first webmaster of *Haiga Online: A Journal of Painting and Poetry* (1998–2002) and is the author of *The Haiku Habit* (Lone Egret Press, 1996), *Barely Dawn* (Lone Egret Press, 1999), *Berries and Cream: Contemporary Haiga in North America* (Press Here, 2000), a book-length interview with Michael Dylan Welch. She has taught haiku, tanka, and haiga at the Loft Literary Center in Minneapolis, Minnesota. Currently, she is the publisher of the annual anthology *Reeds: Contemporary Haiga*, featuring the work of poet-painters from around the world. This is her first collection of tanka poetry.